FANTASTIC PLANETS

The Viking lander descends to the surface of Mars in this pre-launch painting by NASA artist Don Davis. The real lander touched down successfully in July of 1976.

Lunar explorers in George Pal's classic **Destination Moon** *(1950). The landing site pictured here is a careful reproduction of an actual crater on the Moon, although the mud cracks on the ground are a fanciful touch.*

Cyrano de Bergerac chats with the feathered (and quite familiar-looking) inhabitants of the Moon in this illustration from an early edition of **Voyage to the Moon**.

King Dinosaur, *evil ruler of the planet Nova, menaces hapless astronauts in this low-budget film from the 1950s.*

FANTASTIC

By Jean-Claude Suarès and Richard Siegel   Text by David Owen

REED BOOKS

The old and new meet in famed space artist Bob McCall's vision of the future, entitled "Apotheosis of Technology."

*The protagonist of the popular French comic, **The Adventures of Tintin**, discovers one of the effects of the moon's reduced gravitation. This panel is from an episode entitled "Explorers on the Moon." Tintin's adventures are translated into more than a dozen languages.*

PLANETS

The Red Planet is blue and orange, too. In this computer-enhanced photograph produced by the technicians at NASA, Mars's natural coloration is exaggerated in order to heighten contrast.

8

This Softcover original is published by
Reed Books, a division of Addison
House, Inc.

Addison House, Morgan's Run,
Danbury, New Hampshire 03230.
First Edition: 1979
ISBN: 0-89169-534-6
Library of Congress Number: 78-64-553

THE LURE OF OTHER WORLDS

Because the Earth and the creatures that inhabit it are imperfect, we dream of other worlds: places where time stands still, where good is eternally triumphant over evil, where the ground is littered with diamonds and emeralds, where beings more intelligent than ourselves stand ready to tutor us in the ways of peaceful civilization. The petty and the monumental flaws that mar existence in our infinitesimal corner of the universe give rise to visions of extraterrestrial paradises, or of strange and distant hells filled with powerful creatures dedicated to punishing the misdeeds of our inferior species. Even as human beings have viewed themselves as the most powerful and important creatures on Earth, they have also looked to the stars and imagined beings still farther advanced and still more intelligent, and they have placed them in worlds as fantastic as the human imagination can conceive. Those worlds have provided the backgrounds for imaginative works that cover the entire range of creative effort, from great works of literature to Z-grade motion pictures and low-budget fantasy magazines. Whatever the disparities in quality and intention, all such works address a basic human yearning.

For much the greater part of the history of the human race, the Earth itself was a fantastic planet, a mysterious world of uncertain dimensions whose secret places were filled with deities and monsters. Two thousand years ago, members of the most advanced human civilizations believed in the existence of Earth-dwelling gods. These were a race of creatures that could as easily have been described with the catch phrases of modern science fiction: superior beings, advanced intelligences, higher life-forms. As the expanding range of human knowledge narrowed the unknown regions of our planet, Mercury, Venus, Mars, Saturn, Jupiter, and Neptune were forced to vacate terrestrial slopes and take permanent places among the stars; and the longing that led to their creation in the first place urges us to follow them.

The idea that other inhabited worlds exist and even abound is probably as old as those capacities for perception, understanding, and analogy that we think of as being uniquely human. The mythologies of all ancient cultures reflect an overwhelming curiosity about the nature and the arrangement of the stars. The nighttime sky has always presented a tantalizing puzzle. And the attempt to solve it is one of the most profound of all human activities. A measure of its importance can be seen in the fates that befell men who disagreed with the accepted beliefs of their times: In 1600 an Italian monk named Giordano Bruno was burned at the stake, in part for maintaining that the universe was infinite and filled with life-supporting planets.

The universe is the vast background against which we struggle to understand what we are. To speculate about its origin and composition is to speculate about the meaning of human life and to assign it a relative significance on the scale of all that exists. And the problem becomes more complicated every day, as our technological capabilities bring us closer and closer to finding a definite answer. The philosophers of the future may find themselves in the uncomfortable position of having to account in their metaphysics for intelligent beings whose understanding of existence transcends all human notions of morality and justice. Or, every bit as disconcerting, human beings centuries into the future may have to come to terms with the idea that they are, in fact, absolutely alone in the universe. Cosmology is a subject no less vital to our civilization than it was to cultures hundreds or thousands of years ago.

This book deals chiefly with the science-fiction film and with the history of cinematic depiction of other worlds. Such a history is chronicled in the main by frames of celluloid and by the sketches of movie designers, but behind the films themselves lies the ever-changing body of genuine science upon which all science fiction is based. We tend to think of science fiction as a very modern development, but true science has always been accompanied, and

Guides to the stars

*Top: Stanley Kubrick, director of the ultimate science fiction movie, **2001: A space Odyssey** (1968).*

*Middle: J. Allen Hynek, ufologist and technical adviser for **Close Encounters of the Third Kind** (1977).*

Bottom: Wernher Von Braun, founding father of the American space program.

THE LURE OF OTHER WORLDS

sometimes anticipated, by works of speculative fiction arising from a mixture of fact and imagination. The Christian cosmology based on the biblical story of the Creation—a system which was widely accepted as scientifically accurate until relatively recently—is itself a sort of science fiction. The Book of Genesis is the result of an effort by learned men to mold a few known facts into a coherent system by extrapolation and speculation. The modern science-fiction writer performs a similar exercise of the imagination when he expands upon known facts in an effort to arrive, not at the true, but at the possible.

The filmmaker's ability to create and sustain elaborate illusions makes the cinema a natural medium for science fiction, but many important literary works preceded and laid the foundation for the science-fiction film. The scientific revolution of the sixteenth and seventeenth centuries led to the creation of a large number of fanciful works which appeared alongside the scientific ones. Sometimes the science and the fancy were the work of the same author, as in the case of Johannes Kepler, the brilliant seventeenth-century scientist who established the elliptical nature of planetary orbits. Kepler found time also to write the *Somnium (Dream)*, a work of fiction involving life on another world. In the *Somnium*, Kepler is transported to the Moon, where he discovers a primitive race of beings who live mostly in caves beneath the lunar surface. The *Somnium* claimed to be nothing more than a work of fantasy, but the "cave model" for lunar inhabitants enjoyed a fairly long lifetime in the history of speculation about life on the Moon.

Around the middle of the seventeenth century, Cyrano de Bergerac, whose nose was immortalized in Edmond Rostand's play of 1898, wrote two novels dealing with travel to other worlds. In *Voyage to the Moon*, the hero travels into space, first (and unsuccessfully) by attaching to himself a number of containers filled with dew, a material which was presumed to be very light, since every morning the sun drew it up into the air. The voyage is finally made in a "spaceship" powered by firecrackers, although not without the help of a great deal of animal marrow, which the moon attracted. In *History of the States and Empires of the Sun*, Cyrano travels throughout the solar system in a small compartment powered by a crystal.

A Metalunan extravehicular craft speeds away from Earth in Joseph Newman's 1954 film, **This Island Earth**.

Facing page:

A space ship left over from an early submarine flick cruises between Mars and the Earth in a poster for a **very** *low budget fantasy film,* **Space Cruiser Yamato**, *made in Japan.*

THE LURE OF OTHER WORLDS

THE LURE OF OTHER WORLDS

In 1866 Bernard de Fontenelle published a book called *Conversations on the Plurality of Worlds*, a lighthearted fictional dialogue concerning the possible existence of Earth-like worlds elsewhere in the universe. At one point Fontenelle says that "because the *Sun*, which is at present immovable, hath ceased to be a Planet; and that the *Earth*, which moves around him, begins to be one, you will not be surprised to hear, that the *Moon* is an *Earth* like this, and that it is inhabited." Fontenelle later decides that the Moon is unlikely to be inhabited after all, since, among other reasons, it has no atmosphere and no surface water. He concludes his discussion of the Moon by suggesting that, although it is unlikely, life may be possible in lunar caves and crevices, a possibility that was not entirely ruled out by some scientists until the Apollo program. Later in his work Fontenelle throws out some gems of astronomical fantasy: "The climate (of Venus) is very favorable for lovers"; "*Mercury* is the *Bedlam* of the Universe"; and, "*Mars* is not worth the trouble of stopping at him."

One of the most intriguing coincidences in the history of speculation about the solar system occurs in Jonathan Swift's *Gulliver's Travels*, published in 1726. In a section dealing with the airborne island of Lauputa, Swift says that Laputa astronomers have discovered that Mars is accompanied by two small satellites. He then describes the orbits of the satellites, and although his figures are largely inaccurate, they are surprisingly suggestive of the true characteristics of Deimos and Phobos, the actual satellites of the planet. What is surprising is that Mars was not known to have any moons at all until 1877, 150 years after *Gulliver's Travels* was written. Swift's lucky guess has led some people to believe that the Irish satirist was in communication with Martians. It is more probable that he was familiar with an old supposition, supported by Kepler, that the number of moons accompanying the individual planets increased in an orderly manner according to their distance from the Sun. Thus, the Earth has one, Jupiter was thought to have only four, and Mars, which falls between, was presumed to have two.

The idea that intelligent life is scattered throughout the universe was held by many of the greatest minds of the eighteenth century. Immanuel Kant thought it was foolish to believe that the Earth was unique, and he had a great many supporters. Kant, incidentally, made a durable contribution to astronomy with his notion of "island universes" and his nebular theory of the formation of the solar system.

One eighteenth-century astronomer believed that life existed in one of the most unlikely places of all. Sir William Herschel, the man who discovered the planet Uranus, thought that the Sun was inhabited, a view that was shared by Newton. Herschel believed that the Sun's

THE LURE OF OTHER WORLDS

great heat was confined to a shielded outer atmosphere, and that sunspots provided natural windows into a solid interior world. This world was surrounded by a temperate atmosphere like our own.

Herschel's ideas were immensely popular, if only because they were so exotic. An even more exotic theoretician was the philosopher Emanuel Swedenborg, who placed the number of inhabited worlds in the universe at more than 600,000. Swedenborg based his claims on mystic experiences during which, he said, spirits from other worlds visited him and gave him information about the universe. Every planet in the solar system was populated by a distinct kind of being. The inhabitants of the Moon, he said, were dwarves with very large lung-like cavities in their chests to enable them to breathe the rarefied air; the inhabitants of Mercury very much resembled those of Earth, although they were thinner and more simply dressed; Venus was populated by two kinds of men, "those who are mild and humane, and those who are fierce and almost like wild beasts." Although Swedenborg's spirits presumably would have been privy to information about celestial bodies which had not yet been discovered by mere mortals, no mention is made of the inhabitants of Pluto.

Perhaps the most enduring of all exotic theories regarding extraterrestrial life arose from the mistranslation of an Italian word. In 1877, the Italian astronomer Giovanni Schiaparelli detected what appeared to be long, narrow depressions on the surface of Mars. He called these formations *canali*, which in Italian means "channels." When Schiaparelli's studies were translated into English, *canali* was taken to mean "canals," a closely related word but one that has profoundly different implications: Channels are formed by nature; canals are built by men. It became widely assumed that astronomers had discovered conclusive evidence of intelligent life on Mars.

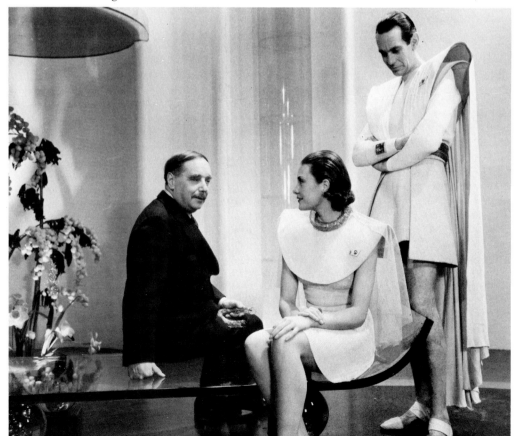

H.G. Wells visits the set of William Cameron Menzies' **Things to Come** *(1936). With Wells are stars Margaretta Scott and Raymond Massey.*

THE LURE OF OTHER WORLDS

THE LURE OF OTHER WORLDS

Intergalactic Hanky-Panky

Facing Page:
High-flying garbage man Adam Quark (Richard Benjamin) is flanked by the Clone Bettys (Cyb and Trish Barnstable) on the set of the TV science-fiction satire **Quark**. *Despite the fact that Buck Henry was its creator, the show barely lasted long enough to be listed in* **TV Guide**.

Left:
Voluptuous space siren **Barbarella** *(Jane Fonda) in the 1967 film of the same name. The popular flick was produced by Dino De Laurentis, directed by Roger Vadim, and based on a French comic strip by Jean-Claude Forrest, who also helped with the screenplay.*

THE LURE OF OTHER WORLDS

Intergalactic Hanky-Panky

Clockwise from above:
Yvonne Craig, TV's Batgirl, as
an insane murderess on **Star**
Trek *episode "Whom Gods*
Destroy"; Yvette Mimieux
grappling with a Morlock in
H.G. Wells' **The Time**
Machine *(1960); Angelique*
Pettyjohn, another **Star Trek**
beauty, in the episode "The
Gamesters of Triskelion."

THE LURE OF OTHER WORLDS

Intergalactic Hanky-Panky

Top: Flash Gordon (*Buster Crabbe*) *rescues Dale Arden* (*Jean Rogers*) *from Ming the Merciless. Note the leftover set from* **The Bride of Frankenstein**.

Bottom:
English actress Caroline Munro, Barbarella without the bubbles, has the lead in this unreleased Italian saga of intrigue in outer space.

THE LURE OF OTHER WORLDS

*Captain Kirk (William Shatner) and his usual band of lieutenants view the time portal in "City on the Edge of Forever," a popular **Star Trek** episode written by noted writer Harlan Ellison.*

The American astronomer Percival Lowell was captivated by the idea of Martian canals. He made his own telescopic studies of the planet and drew maps of what he believed to be an elaborate irrigation system. Lowell theorized that Mars was drying up, and that its inhabitants had constructed canals to exploit the limited water resources remaining in their polar ice caps. Lowell even claimed to be able to detect green "oases" at the intersections of the canals.

Anyone who has seen the photographs of the surface of Mars that were taken by the Viking cameras will wonder what all the fuss was about. Mars is a dusty planet that looks very much like the Moon and very little like a highly engineered environment. We know now that Lowell's canals were actually a combined product of his eager imagination and the impossibility of gaining a precise telescopic view of the Martian surface. The atmosphere of the Earth and Mars, and the vast distance involved, blur widely separated and irregular features and can make them appear to be more uniform than they really are. Some of Lowell's canals were actually long chains of mountains. Others existed nowhere but in his imagination.

Roughly contemporary with Lowell was a man whose fantasies about other worlds took an entirely different form. This was Georges Méliès, a French film director who in 1902 produced what is generally agreed to be the first science-fiction film ever made, the classic *A Trip to the Moon*. Based loosely on Jules Verne's *From the Earth to the Moon* and H. G. Wells's *First Men in the Moon*, Méliès's film is a brief, though rollicking, silent feature which employs some of the most imaginative visual effects available at the time in portraying a story which does not try very hard to maintain the semblance of scientific authority. In Méliès's vision, the Moon is covered with gigantic mushroom-like plants and is inhabited by an ugly race of beings called Selenites. The principal features of the lunar surface are the eyes, nose, and mouth of the familiar Man in the Moon, and in one darkly comic scene, the Man in the

THE LURE OF OTHER WORLDS

Moon's right eye provides the landing pad for a rocket ship full of Earthlings.

Méliès's visual effects are undeniably crude, and if his film has any real appeal today it is probably as camp. The technological dexterity that fascinates modern science-fiction-film viewers—the brilliantly achieved special effects of *2001: A Space Odyssey* or *Star Wars*—is present only at the very most primitive stage. But Méliès's intention was not the same as Stanley Kubrick's or George Lucas's, and it might not have been even if he had had access to the visual tricks of the modern director; what Méliès had first in mind was to adapt the techniques of theatrical drama and burlesque to the special demands of a new medium. Thus it is a chorus line of dancing girls, and not a group of scientists, who prepare his rocket ship for lift-off. What is interesting to us is that he chose for his experiment a subject which we justly think of as belonging to science fiction.

Celluloid turns to dust as quickly as the flesh, and for that reason we know some old films only from contemporary descriptions or from surviving set designs and stills. One such film is *Algol*, made in 1920 by the German director Hans Werkmeister. No print of the film survives, but fragmentary stills reveal its set, which depicted the surface of a world called Algol, to have been a spectacular creation. Directors and designers were clearly making an effort to move beyond visual triteness that infected Méliès set for *A Trip to the Moon*. Filmmakers were applying the same imaginative energy to producing backgrounds for their works as they were to conceiving of fanciful space vehicles and alien monsters.

Of course, difficulties of scale limit any filmmaker in the creation of full-scale physical environments; it is easy to dress a stunt man as a bug-eyed monster or to create a spaceship from a few lengths of metal tubing, but it is difficult—and expensive—to convert entire landscapes into exotic locales. Even in such a highly budgeted and technologically expert film as *Star Wars*, the creatures and vehicles receive more decorative attention than the terrain. The aliens in the celebrated bar scene are worth every penny that it took to create them, but the surface of Tatooine, even with a double sun overhead, never manages to look very different from the Tunisian desert where it was filmed. To some extent, the filmmaker's challenge is to make the viewer belive that something very familiar is in fact something very exotic. Small touches can suggest much more than they represent in and of themselves.

Destination Moon, a film that ushered in the American science-fiction boom of the 1950s, strove for realism in all of its estimable visual details. Ernest Fegté designed the set with some help from the Mount Wilson Observatory, and artist Chesley Bonestell painted it. The film's director, George Pal, was so intent on realism that the moon set was a careful copy of a

The alien mother ship hovers over the secret landing platform on Devil's Tower in the thrilling climax of Steven Spielberg's blockbuster, **Close Encounters of the Third Kind***.*

THE LURE OF OTHER WORLDS

Far Out Fashions

Top left: *The dapper alien Klaatu (Michael Rennie(and his metallic companion Gort face frightened Earthlings in* **The Day the Earth Stood Still** *(1951.) Gort's robot suit is made of foam rubber sprayed silver.*

Top right: *Spock (Leonard Nimoy) models Enterprise fatigues accented by a long sash at the waist.*

Bottom: *Apollo II astronauts Armstrong, Collins and Aldrin sporting the real thing. The design of NASA's space suits has always been influenced in numerous small and large ways by costumes created for the movies.*

THE LURE OF OTHER WORLDS

Far Out Fashions

Buck Rogers (Buster Crabbe) *in his 25th-century jumpsuit, flanked by Saturian royalty in appropriate fashions. The woman clutching Buck's arm is Wilma Deering (Constance Moore.)*

Above: Flash Gordon Conquers the Universe *in his Errol Flynn-style clothes. At his side is Dale Arden (Jean Rogers), who looks a little like a cross between Robin Hood and an airline stewardess.*

THE LURE OF OTHER WORLDS

real lunar crater, and the Earth visible in the darkness beyond it was in precisely the position it would have been in if the film actually had been shot "on location." As a result, *Destination Moon* is a film of remarkable technical accomplishment, even though most viewers never realized the great care that had been devoted to particular details. The finished product pales in comparison with more recent space extravaganzas, but Pal's accomplishment is nonetheless remarkable, and it set a new standard for realism.

Science-fiction writer Robert A. Heinlein, who served as technical adviser for the film, described some of the pains taken to insure the realism of the production: "As shooting progressed we began to be deluged with visitors of technical background—guided-missile men, astronomers, rocket engineers, aircraft engineers. The company, seeing that their work was being taken seriously by technical specialists, took pride in turning out an authentic job. There were no more remarks of 'What difference does it make?'"

The members of Pal's film company were not the only ones to benefit from their working relationship with scientists; the scientists themselves went away from production meetings with new ideas, some of which were eventually applied to the space program. One of these, a portable propulsion device using compressed air, was used by the first astronauts who walked in space.

In the category of realism, Stanley Kubrick's masterful *2001: A Space Odyssey* takes all the prizes. Even an expert might have trouble distinguishing Kubrick's Moon set from NASA photos of the real thing. Kubrick had tremendously sophisticated technology at his disposal, but machines alone do not make movies: The brilliance of *2001* is more than anything a tribute to the patience and the inventiveness of the people who put it together. Months of planning and hours of shooting time were spent in producing mere snippets of finished film, and the result is a technical achievement which even *Star Wars* and *Close Encounters of the*

A NASA artist's conception of a manned base that may one day be constructed on the surface of the Moon. The buildings in this picture are located near the lunar south pole, and the architecture is modeled on stations in Antarctica. The contraption peeking around the right-hand edge of the drawing is an Apollo-style lunar lander.

THE LURE OF OTHER WORLDS

Third Kind do not really rival. And supporting Kubrick's effects is what can only be described as a masterful creative vision. The movie's script, written by Kubrick and science-fiction writer Arthur C. Clarke, is every bit as "experimental" as the visual effects. *Star Wars* is merely an oversized comic book fleshed out with million-dollar effects, but *2001* is an entity unto itself.

Despite the advances in film technology in the last decade, Kubrick's film still undisputedly represents the pinnacle of achievement in science fiction cinema. *2001* manages to be both a movie about technology and an extremely remarkable example of that technology itself. It is in part from this that the movie derives its power. The film's creators and their techniques bear the same sort of relationship to each other as the Ape Man and his crude weapon, the scientists and their computer Hal, or the extraterrestrials and their mysterious monoliths. The movie *is* the future, a rough synthesis of the conflict between man and machine.

*The surprisingly authentic-looking Moonbase from TV's popular **Space: 1999**.*

Realism is not the only goal in science-fiction cinema; it is not even the major one. Once again, the reason is partly economic: It costs a great deal of money to make an exact copy of a part of the Moon, or to create a plausible rendering of real but only vaguely understood worlds. And as advances in genuine space technology fill in gaps in our understanding of space, the act of imagining the unknown becomes a little less difficult, and the urge to do so becomes less intense. When *Destination Moon* was filmed, we had no direct knowledge of the surface of the Moon, and the filmmaker's challenge was to make the best educated guess possible, to decide what the Moon *must* be like. Today we know what the Moon *is* like, and in such a situation the task of the director who wishes to set his movie on the Moon is transformed. The knowledge brought by our forays into space has changed the fabric of science-fiction cinema. The recent release *Capricorn I*, for example, is not a story about the planet Mars, but rather a story about simulation of the planet Mars. It is a science-fiction movie whose subject is science fiction.

*A long shot of the landing pad in **Close Encounters of the Third Kind**. In this scene compact shuttle vehicles are giving Devil's Tower the once-over before allowing the mother ship to land.*

The comic book has had a vast influence on the science-fiction film. *Flash Gordon, Buck Rogers, Barbarella, Star Wars*, and others all derive from the comics, with the resulting emphasis on innocent heroes, beautiful girls, horrifying monsters, and outlandish sets. Flash Gordon was the first to forsake the limiting frames of the Sunday funny pages for the wider

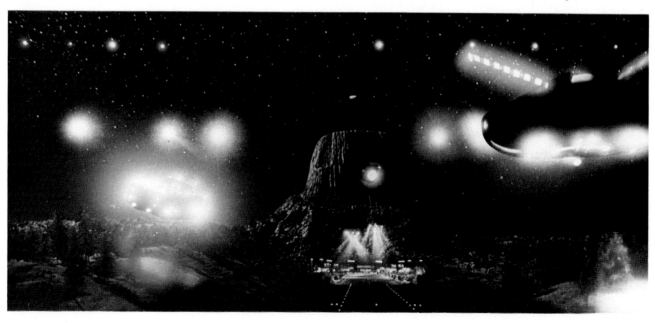

THE LURE OF OTHER WORLDS

horizons of the Hollywood screen, but others soon followed. The sappy formula derived from the Gordon serial provided the basis for dozens of imitations.

The vast majority of science-fiction films—the low-budget, low-quality horror movies that came into their own in the 1950s and remain popular on the drive-in circuit today—concern themselves not so much with other worlds as with the inhabitants of those worlds. New monsters constructed from the discarded parts of old ones followed one another on and off the screen, and the same old arid desert locations were passed from one production to the next. A few of the monsters and their homes have been memorable, but all belong to a different discussion.

Television science fiction is a less fully developed genre than its cinematic counterpart, but there are a few notable shows. The ever-popular *Star Trek* offered, and continues to offer through reruns, its odd assortment of alien worlds which manage to look pretty much alike despite distinguishing features here and there. The most technically accomplished of all sci-fi TV shows was the short-lived *Space: 1999*, whose Moonbase Alpha set was a genuine achievement.

When the world entered the Space Age two decades ago, speculation about other worlds began to take on a new and serious meaning. Films of other worlds began to be produced by the very serious scientists at NASA's simulation laboratories. At an amazingly rapid rate, mankind was developing the scientific means for actually settling some of history's most

*Barbie-doll-like beauties line the mazes that lead to the capital city of filth and disgust in **Barbarella** (1967.)*

THE LURE OF OTHER WORLDS

An expedition to Mars ends in a tangle with evil aliens who live in a world of sand in the "Invisible Enemy" episode of **The Outer Limits.**

The First Men in the Moon *examine bizarre local flora beneath the lunar surface. This 1964 remake of the 1919 classic was produced by Charles Schneer. Special effects were provided by Ray Harryhausen.*

THE LURE OF OTHER WORLDS

fantastic notions about the universe. In many ways, the astonishing rate of scientific progress in the recent past is every bit as amazing as the distant civilizations our instruments may one day enable us to detect and perhaps to visit.

Mars has always seemed to be an especially promising planet on which to look for life. Its size and general characteristics are roughly comparable to those of the Earth, and it is close enough to make detailed observation, and perhaps even manned exploration, possible. Even without canals, Mars looks like a place that might reasonably be expected to support some kind of life.

About twenty years ago, the Russian astronomer I. S. Shklovskii proposed that Mars might in fact support an incredibly advanced form of life. Shklovskii's hypothesis was not the work of fancy; it was the result of careful and precise scientific observations, and it suggested that the moons of Mars, mentioned earlier in connection with Jonathan Swift, might actually be huge artificial satellites. Shklovskii's argument is much too technical to reproduce here, but in general it was based upon certain apparent anomalies in the orbit of one of the moons. Phobos was behaving as though it weighed much less than other observations showed it should. The only way to account for the orbital peculiarity, Shklovskii concluded, was to presume that Phobos was hollow. And Phobos could only be hollow if it had been created by other than natural forces. Perhaps the surviving remnant of an ancient Martian civilization was living inside its ample ten-mile diameter.

Shklovskii's proposal was highly controversial, but it was consistent with the known facts about the satellites and no scientist was able to prove it wrong. There even seemed to be some historical support for the idea: The moons of Mars were not discovered until 1877, even though the planet had been observed carefully fifteen years before with a telescope theoretically capable of seeing them. Not only were Phobos and Deimos behaving like artificial satellites, they even seemed to have an identifiable "launch date."

We now know that Phobos is not the final outpost of an advanced civilization. Its seemingly inconsistent characteristics can be accounted for by other explanations. Still, Phobos would be an interesting place to visit. Its gravitational force is only about one tenth of one percent of that of the Earth. As Carl Sagan pointed out in *The Cosmic Connection*, "If you can perform a standing high jump of two or three feet on Earth, you could perform a standing high jump of half a mile on Phobos."

As for life on Mars itself, scientists are still fairly uncertain. The two Viking landers that conducted biological detection experiments on its surface in 1976 transmitted back a great deal of data which are open to a wide range of interpretation. Some of the experiments seemed to indicate that life processes are taking place, others seemed to rule them out. We will not be able to come to a final decision until a lander with broader capabilities can make a more

*"The Doomsday Machine" from the **Star Trek** episode of the same name prepares to engulf another planetary system in its deadly search for energy.*

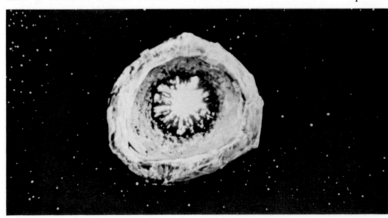

THE LURE OF OTHER WORLDS

*A storm trooper riding beastback on the deserts of Tatooine searches for loitering droids in this scene from **Star Wars**.(1977).*

*Darth Vader's uncle? Luke Skywalker's number one enemy bears a striking resemblance to this creature, who appeared in an illustration in **Analog** magazine long before Darth was born.*

THE LURE OF OTHER WORLDS

definitive investigation.

It may also be possible that life once existed upon Mars but has since died out or been confined to isolated niches in the environment. Satellite photographs of the surface of the planet reveal huge formations which scientists believe could only have been formed by the eroding action of running water. Mars may once have been much more like the Earth than it is today. It could even conceivably turn out to be a fossil hunter's paradise.

Venus was once thought to be capable of supporting Earth-like life, but scientists are now certain that it is not. For one thing, its surface temperature is about 475 degrees centigrade, which is hot enough to fry any organism on Earth. Some scientists believe that life may exist (or could be "planted") in the cooler regions of the upper atmosphere, but the amorous Venusians of Fontenelle are out of the question.

Elsewhere in the solar system, the prospects of finding life of any kind are bleak. Mercury is too hot (photographs of its surface show that it looks a great deal like the Moon) and the outer planets are more like balls of gas than anything we are accustomed to think of as "worlds." There is a possibility, though, that Titan, one of the numerous moons that orbit Saturn beyond its rings, may be life-supporting. Titan has an atmosphere and its surface conditions seem to resemble those of the Earth at the stage when life was just beginning.

But beyond the solar system altogether, it seems not only possible but even *likely* that life, and even life "as we know it," exists. A great many astronomers, in fact, will tell you that it is almost a certainty.

We have no direct knowledge of the universe beyond our solar system, but the incredibly sensitive instruments now available to astronomers have given us a fairly clear picture of what it is like. And what it is like, surprisingly enough, is not entirely unfamiliar. This does not mean that the universe is without strange and inexplicable marvels. It merely means, as astronomers are fond of saying, that the Earth orbits an average star in an average section of an average galaxy. Statistical calculations even indicate that there may be *billions* of life-supporting planets within our own Milky Way. And when we consider that the Milky Way is only an average galaxy, that number must be increased by still more billions to include the rest of the universe. It would be surprising indeed if there were *no* life anywhere else in the universe; the chance of our being alone would seem to be almost too small to compute.

Some astronomers are beginning to think, however, that the abundance of Earth-like planets in the universe is significantly lower than has previously been supposed. It may be,

One of the monsters that tormented **Flesh Gordon** *(Jason Williams, 1972).*

THE LURE OF OTHER WORLDS

for instance, that viable planet systems are formed only in conjunction with such relatively rare phenomena as supernovae. Still, the likelihood of extraterrestrial life remains almost inconceivably large.

In the last twenty years or so, astronomers have been actively searching for evidence of civilizations elsewhere in the universe. The principal tool they have been using in their search is the radio telescope, which is an instrument that detects radio waves in roughly the same way that an optical telescope detects light waves. The advantage of a radio telescope is that it can be made much larger, and hence more powerful, than an optical telescope: A radio telescope is made of wires, while a traditional telescope depends on mirrors or lenses, the size of which is limited by the intricate technologies involved in producing them. In hypothetical terms, a radio telescope could be as big as we wanted it to be.

Some of the astronomers who are scanning the skies with radio telescopes are hoping to detect a signal from a distant civilization that has developed radio capability and has decided to see if anyone else has reached a similar level of advancement. Astronomers would be able to recognize such a signal by its regularity or by some other feature which would distinguish it from the radio waves that other objects in space produce naturally. Even if an advanced civilization were not transmitting such a signal, we would be able to detect it anyway, given that local communication was taking place on radio frequencies. Even though no one on Earth is transmitting a greeting signal into space, a radio astronomer on Mars, for instance, would be able to deduce our presence from the abnormally large amount of radiation that our television stations, radar installations, and other transmitters broadcast into space in all directions every minute of every day.

The first systematic radio search for extraterrestrial life was initiated by Frank Drake in 1960. The project was called Ozma, in honor of *The Wizard of Oz*, and it has been followed by several others. Today, a few radio telescopes around the world regularly devote small parts of their "listening" time to the search for extraterrestrial life.

A very different project related to a different kind of extraterrestrial life has been gathering interest recently. This is the "space colony" program proposed by Gerard O'Neill, a professor at Princeton. O'Neill's proposal involves the construction, mostly in space, of a huge space "city" which would orbit the Earth and house perhaps as many as 10,000 people. One of the colony's principal functions would be to beam solar energy to receiving centers on the Earth, and O'Neill looks forward to a day when thousands of such colonies will provide homes for the excess population of our planet. O'Neill has attracted a number of nearly worshipful followers who dream of the "simpler" life to be had aboard the orbiting cities. No one seems to have considered, though, that a child born in even the most luxurious space colony might very well decide that the vast and beautiful planet orbiting outside the window looked like a much more interesting place to live.

When and if we do discover intelligent life on another planet, the way we think about ourselves and our universe will be profoundly and permanently changed. What course that change will take will depend upon how human beings are able to adjust to a picture of the universe that may no longer place them at the pinnacle of existence. But even if we should come into contact with a civilization advanced beyond us by millions of years, that discovery need not diminish our estimation of our true significance. As the astronomer Harlow Shapley wrote in *Of Stars and Men*, "Are we debased by the greater speed of the sparrow, the larger size of the hippopotamus, the keener hearing of the dog, the finer detectors of odor possessed by insects? We can easily get adjusted to all of these evidences of our inferiority and maintain a feeling of importance and well-being. We should adjust to the cosmic facts. It is a magnificent universe in which to play a part, however humble."

CHAPTER ONE
THE MOON

As the Earth's closest and most visible celestial neighbor, the Moon has been the subject of a substantial share of man's speculation about the existence of extraterrestrial worlds. Galileo's discovery that the Moon is not a perfect crystal sphere but rather an Earth-like body with a rough and varied terrain, opened new doors to the imagination. From the playful fictions of Cyrano and Verne to the pseudoscientific nonsense propounded by would-be-serious men, the Moon has provided ample inspiration for human fantasy.

The cratered lunar landscape has also inspired settings for numerous science fiction movies, and not only for those intended to take place on the moon. Lunar craters are ubiquitous as adornments to movie sets, and indeed the surfaces of some very real planets—Mercury, for example—look very much like Earth's familiar satellite.

After George Méliès introduced the Moon to the screen in *A Trip to the Moon*, a host of imitations followed. In the early years of the motion picture, titles like *Moon Man, Moonstruck, The Man in the Moon*, and *When the Man in the Moon Seeks a Wife* were fairly common. More recently, though, the Moon-in-the-Movies has been supplanted by more exotic locales which allow for more exciting visual effects and more colorful indigenous populations.

*Alien interloper attacks the SHADO moonbase in the television series **UFO**.*

Facing Page:
Artist Tom Kowal's Verne-inspired conception of the Sun being eclipsed by the Earth as seen from the Moon.

TRIP TO THE MOON —

— LE

*A pre-production sketch for Georges Méliès' **A Trip to the Moon** (1914) showing the Earthlings' spaceship lodged in the eye of the Man in the Moon.*

Above: *The film realization of the scene at left.*

*An astro-cat drifts around the bullet-like space capsule in this illustration from Jules Verne's **From the Earth to the Moon**.*

*A similar-looking spacecraft from Fritz Lang's masterpiece **Frau im Mond** (1929).*

The **First Men
in the Moon** (1964) leave
their elaborate spherical space
pod and descend to the lunar
surface.

THE SHELL REACHES THE MOON

*Two spectacular pre-production sketches for **A Trip to the Moon**, the Georges Méliès masterpiece that is generally agreed to be the first science-fiction movie ever made. In the drawing above, an astronaut with a telescope and, of all things, an umbrella focuses in on the rings of Saturn after crashing his space shell on the lunar surface. Depicted in the drawing at left are the lobster-like Selenites, inhabitants of the Earth's satellite.*

Au clair de la lune,
 Nous irons s'il faut,
Jusqu'à Pampelune,
 Bâtir des châteaus !

La Favorite
2453/4
Visé-Paris

This French fantasy postcard from the turn of the century may very well have inspired Méliès. If the Man in the Moon knows what's good for him, he'll keep his eyes closed.

"THE MOON DOOM"
by Nathaniel Salisbury

Facing page: *Artist Alex Schomburg's rendition of a manned lunar base. The drawing appeared in a 1952 edition of* **Startling Stories**, *a pulp science-fiction magazine.*

Above: *A runaway moon creates huge tidal waves on the Earth in this cover illustration for "The Moon Doom" by Nathaniel Salisbury, which appeared in Hugo "The Father of Science Fiction" Gernsback's* **Wonder Stories**.

Footprints on the Moon

Tintin makes his mark on the lunar surface in this panel from "Explorer on the Moon" in Hergé's **The Adventures of Tintin**.

Below: *The real thing. An Apollo astronaut's footprint on the Moon. Because there is no such thing as lunar weather, the footprint will remain exactly as it is in the picture for thousands of years—unless a meteor lands on it or a housing project goes up over it.*

Facing page: *An Apollo II astronaut salutes his country's flag. A metal bar extending from the pole keeps the banner from hanging limp, as it would if it were to look after itself.*

A small step for a man . . .

The astronauts in George Pal's
Destination Moon (1950)
make their initial descent to the
lunar surface (left) the same
way that Buzz Aldrin did
two decades later (above).

At home on the Moon

*Three visions of men on the Moon. Above is a scene from **Destination Moon**. At left is a Soviet artist's rendition of a proposed lunar base.*

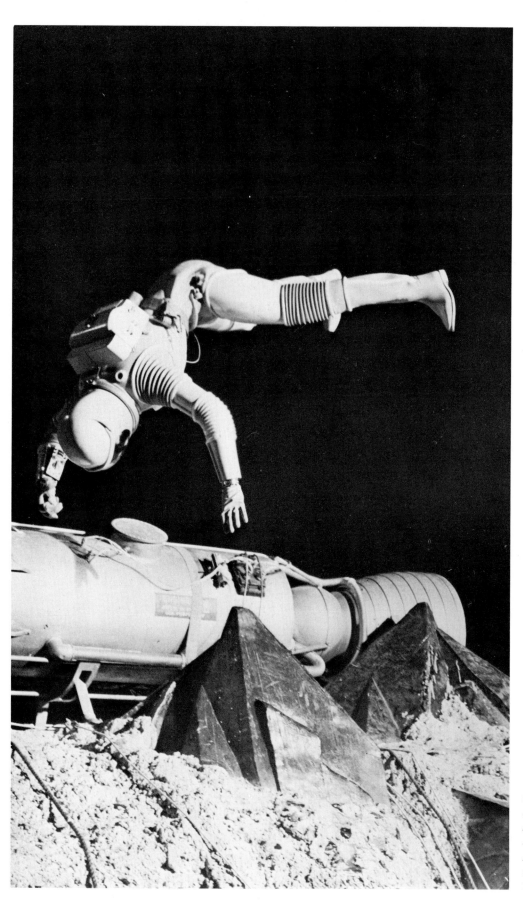

A scene from **Moon Zero-Two**, *the world's first space western.*

Overleaf: *A space shuttle dispatched from the orbiting space station in* **2001** *sets down on the surface of the Moon. The craft was designed by special effects man Douglas Trumbull.*

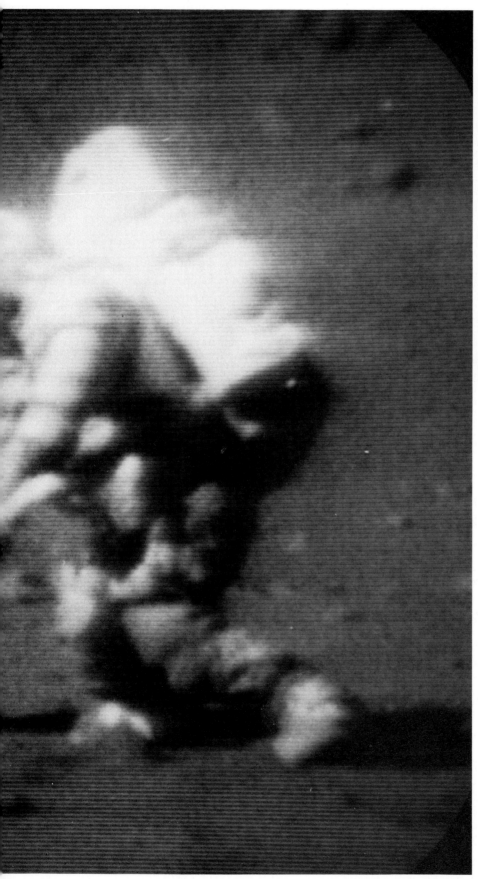

*Cavor (Lionel Jeffries) tangles with a pair of dastardly Selenites in **First Men in the Moon**.*

The Apollo II astronauts gather Moon rocks with shovels provided by the designers at NASA.

Two NASA pictures, one a simulation, the other real. At left is an artist's conception of a lunar module on its way to the Moon. Above is the actual Apollo II module, "The Eagle," piloted by Neil Armstrong and Buzz Aldrin. This picture was taken by Michael Collins, who remained in orbit aboard the command module.

Space 1999.

Above is a look behind the scenes on the set of the television series Space: 1999: Special effects wizard Bryan Johnston, who will also be responsible for the effects in the **Star Wars** *sequel, stands among his marvellously detailed miniatures on the TV sound stage. At left, three representatives of the lunar Red Cross carry medical supplies to wounded astronauts.*

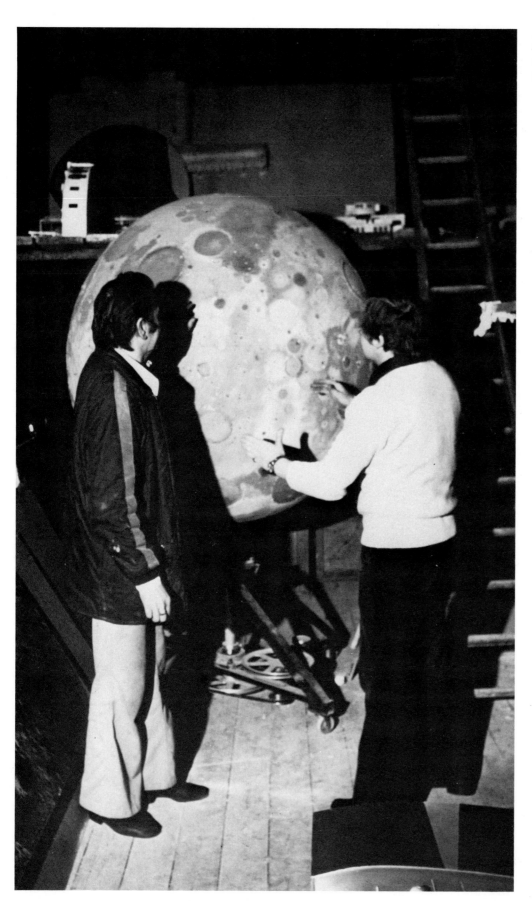

Johnston puts finishing touches on the model of the Moon that he created for the show.

Artist Bob McCall's huge mural celebrating the Apollo program. The painting is on display at the Air and Space Museum of the Smithsonian Institution in Washington.

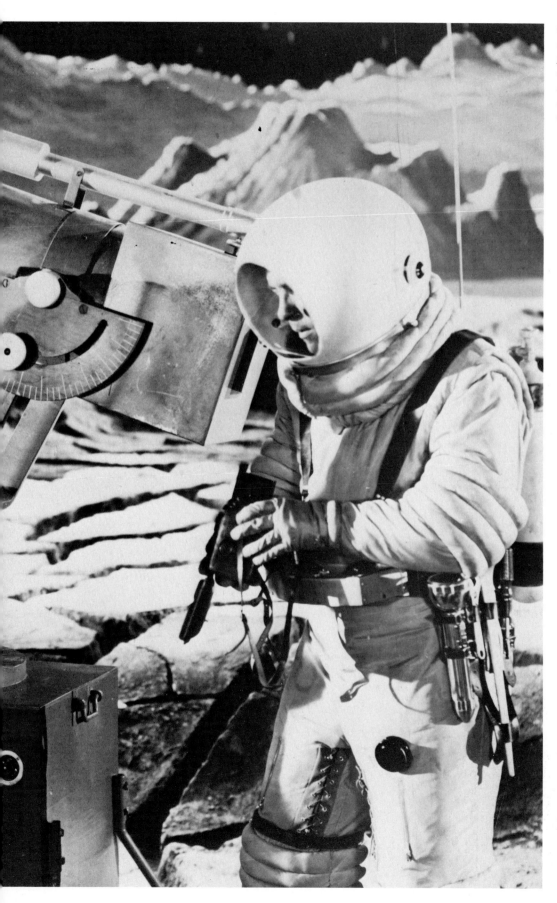

One of the astronauts in **Destination Moon** *(1950) positions his hand so that it will appear to be supporting Earth in a photograph taken by his companion. Even space travelers act like tourists.*

*John Schoenher's cover painting for **Analog** magazine. The picture illustrates a scene from Frank Herbert's masterpiece, **Dune**.*

*The Oz-like citadel at left is part of a matte painting used as a set on the "Menagerie" episode of **Star Trek**.*

Left: *An Apollo space craft above the surface of the Moon.*

Above: *A shootout at the lunar corral from* **Moon Zero-Two**.

Two covers from the fantasy **Weird Science**. On the facing page is Wally Wood's depiction of the first encounter between man and an intelligent life form from another planet. Another Wood illustration, this time a winged intergalactic terror menaces the classic hero and heroine.
© 1979 by William M. Gaines

Space Odyssey
*Two shots from Stanley Kubrick's **2001**. Above, the dome-like moonport opens to receive a lunar shuttle, which is approaching the lunar surface in the picture below.*

The spectacular mother ship hovers above Devil's Tower in **Close Encounters**. It would not be polite to ask how much it cost to produce this scene.

Lunar archaeologists uncover a monolith on the Moon in **2001**.

MARS

When cinematic fictions about the Moon began to wear thin, moviemakers turned to the mysterious red planet. Mars, with its supposed network of irrigation canals and its presumably intelligent race of master builders, was the perfect location for a screenwriter with a bent for science fiction.

Indeed, Mars has probably been the subject of more works of science fiction—reaching at least as far back as Swift and *Gulliver's Travels*—than all the other planets put together. Mars's major qualification is the fact that it is close enough to the Earth to be observed, but far enough away so that the details of its appearance were left, until very recently, to the imagination of its observers. Over the years, the term "Martian" has been used to describe a range of imaginary beings almost as varied as the species that inhabit the Earth.

A substantial number of cinematic Martians have been portrayed not on their native ground but as invaders of the Earth, as in *The War of the Worlds* and a host of others. But Mars itself appears from time to time, and one of its classic appearances is in *Flash Gordon's Trip to Mars*, which was filmed in 1938.

Simulation of a Mars landing in Sir Lew Grade's thriller **Capricorn One** *(1978). The shot is a parody of a famous Moon photograph.*

Facing page: *Warfare on Mars as imagined by noted fantasy artist Jeff Kronen.*

Lunar archaeologists uncover a monolith on the Moon in **2001**.

MARS

When cinematic fictions about the Moon began to wear thin, moviemakers turned to the mysterious red planet. Mars, with its supposed network of irrigation canals and its presumably intelligent race of master builders, was the perfect location for a screenwriter with a bent for science fiction.

Indeed, Mars has probably been the subject of more works of science fiction—reaching at least as far back as Swift and *Gulliver's Travels*—than all the other planets put together. Mars's major qualification is the fact that it is close enough to the Earth to be observed, but far enough away so that the details of its appearance were left, until very recently, to the imagination of its observers. Over the years, the term "Martian" has been used to describe a range of imaginary beings almost as varied as the species that inhabit the Earth.

A substantial number of cinematic Martians have been portrayed not on their native ground but as invaders of the Earth, as in *The War of the Worlds* and a host of others. But Mars itself appears from time to time, and one of its classic appearances is in *Flash Gordon's Trip to Mars*, which was filmed in 1938.

Simulation of a Mars landing in Sir Lew Grade's thriller **Capricorn One** *(1978). The shot is a parody of a famous Moon photograph.*

Facing page: *Warfare on Mars as imagined by noted fantasy artist Jeff Kronen.*

Above and left: *Thark rides a Thoat in these animation drawings by Bob Clampett for a proposed cartoon series featuring Edgar Rice Burroughs's immortal* **John Carter of Mars.**

Facing page: *This episode of* **Little Nemo in Slumberland** *by Winsor McCay pokes fun at monopolies on Mars. The ubiquitous B. Gosh & Co. seems to have bought up every last square inch of the Martian surface.*

(John Carter of Mars © 1978 by Edgar Rice Burroughs, Inc. Illustration © 1978 by Bob Clampett. World rights reserved.)

The Red Planet

Three views of Mars. Above is a frame from a NASA film about the planet. The film is an animated simulation based on real photographs provided by the Mariner 9 probe, which charted Mars in 1972. Pictured is the Caldera Nix Olympica, the largest known crater in the solar system. At left is artist Don Davis's conception of a Viking lander touching down on Mars. On the facing page is a computer-enhanced photo of Mars from the Viking mission.

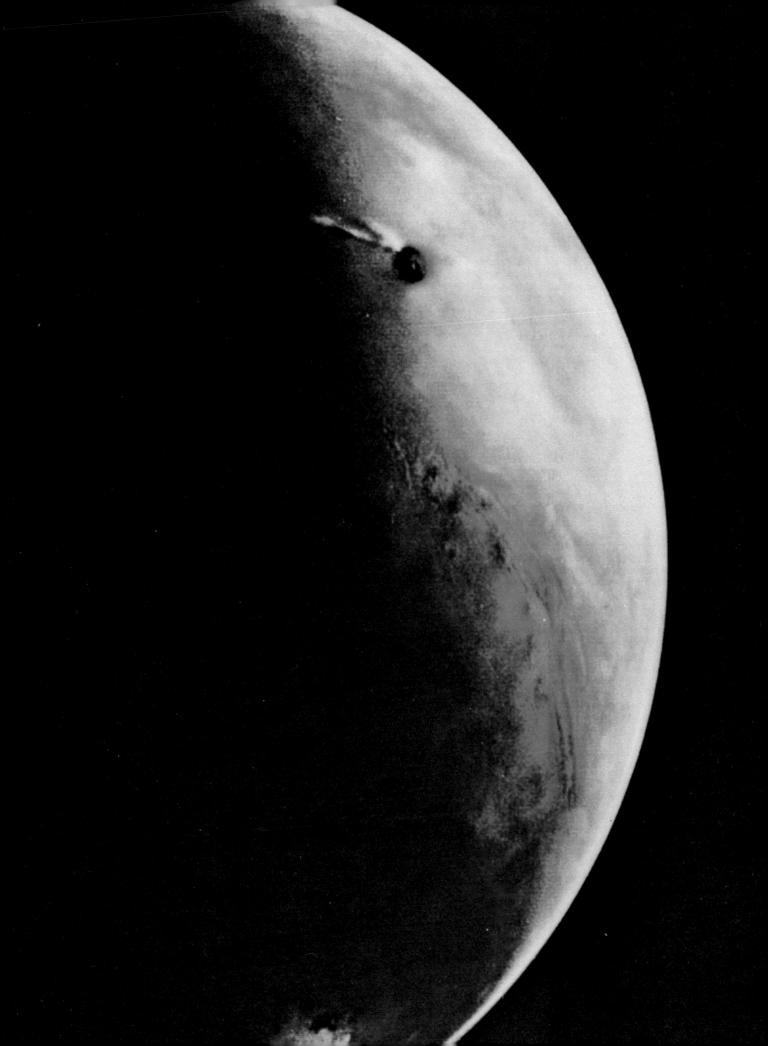

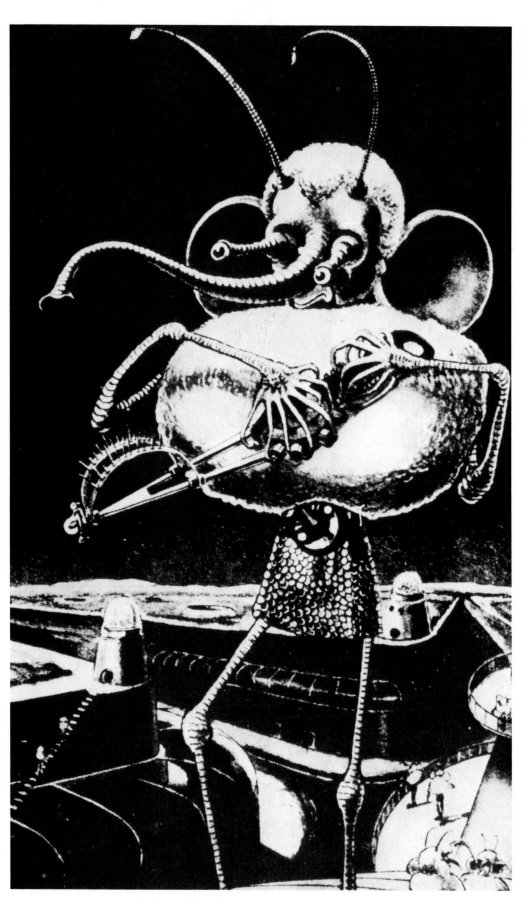

Facing page: A painting of Mars by Hannes Bok from a 1974 issue of **Famous Fantastic Mysteries**.

Left: An illustration by Frank R. Paul for "The Martian," a story that appeared in **Science Fiction Plus**.

The spectacular Martian sunset as photographed by Viking. The photograph was taken in sections as Viking's camera scanned 120 degrees of the horizon. Colors in the sky are caused by particles suspended in the air, just as they are on Earth.

Flash Gordon's Trip to Mars
Left:
Flash Gordon (Buster Crabbe)
confers with the King of the
Clay People, rightful ruler of
Mars, in **Flash Gordon's**
Trip to Mars *(1938).*

Flash turns the tables on Ming
the Merciless.

Azura, the evil witch queen of Mars, prepares to restore the Clay People to their normal, human form, per instructions from Flash.

Two illustrations by Reed Crandall. **Facing page:** John Carter leaps to safety over the heads of the great white apes of Mars. **Left:** Carter prepares to rescue his beloved princess. Dejah Thoris, and his Thark pal, Tars Tarkas (John Carter of Mars © 1978 by Edgar Rice Burroughs, Inc. World rights reserved.)

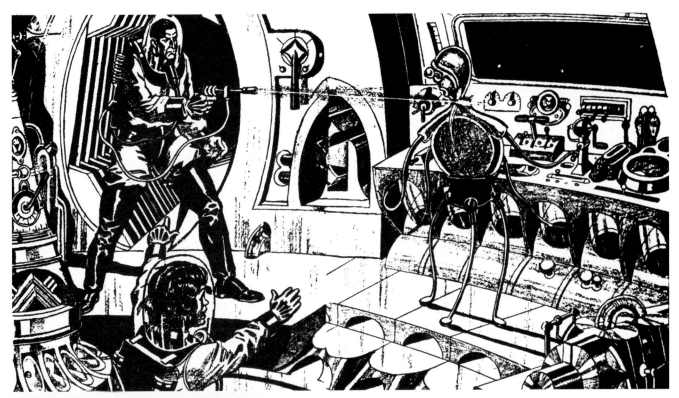

Happiness is a warm raygun

No space explorer would be complete without his pocket disintegrator. Above is a Marchioni illustration for "Child of the Stars," a story by Raymond A. Gallun which appeared in a 1936 issue of **Astounding Stories**. *At left, a sensuous maiden is energized by a wide-eyed lizard in a Virgil Finlay illustration for a 1943 edition of* **Famous Fantastic Mysteries**. *On the facing page, a brace of hand-blasters make short work of three spear-carrying space bears. The illustration is from* **Planet Stories**, *yet another fantasy pulp.*

BRAVE AND BOLD WEEKLY

Issued Weekly. By subscription $2.50 per year. Entered according to Act of Congress in the year 1907, in the Office of the Librarian of Congress, Washington, D. C., by STREET & SMITH, 79-89 Seventh Avenue, New York, N. Y.

No. 256   NEW YORK, NOVEMBER 16, 1907.   **Price, Five Cents**

AT WAR WITH MARS

——— OR ———

The Boys Who Won

BY WELDON J. COBB

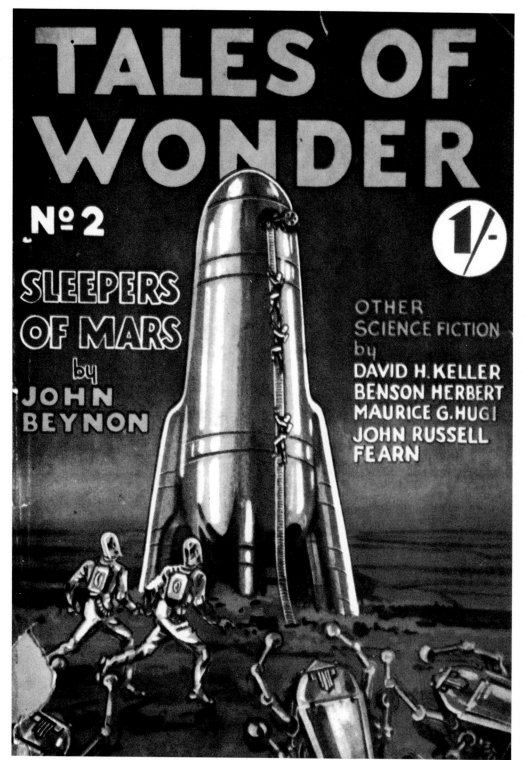

The cover of **Tales of Wonder**, No. 2. **SLEEPERS OF MARS** by **JOHN BEYNON**. No 2. 1/-. OTHER SCIENCE FICTION by **DAVID H. KELLER**, **BENSON HERBERT**, **MAURICE G. HUGI**, **JOHN RUSSELL FEARN**.

Facing page: A malevolent missile from Mars eyeballs the Earth in Weldon J. Cobb's painting for the cover of the **Brave and Bold Weekly**.

Left: The cover of **Tales of Wonder**.

Space Travel

Above: *A pair of space travelers court danger on a voyage to the beyond.*

Left: *Harry Grant Dart's painting for the cover of the "Life on Mars" number of the old* **Life** *magazine. Never mind that wings don't belong on space ships.*

Two Wally Wood paintings for covers of **Weird Science**. In both illustrations, astronauts of one breed or another come face to face with the evil that seems to lurk in just about every corner of the universe.

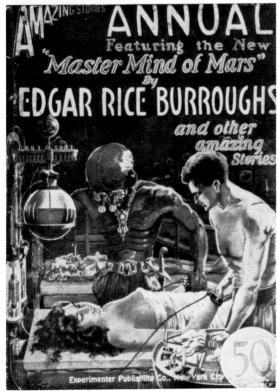

Above: *Illustration by Frank Frazetta for the cover of the* **Famous Funnies** *edition of Buck Rogers' adventures.*

Left: *Painting by Frank R. Paul for Edgar Rice Burroughs' story, "Mastermind of Mars," which deals with test-tube Martians.*
© 1979 by Edgar Rice Burroughs, Inc. World Rights Reserved

An axe-toting Martian Amazon slashes her way through T. Anderson's cover illustration for a story by the late Leigh Brackett, who wrote the screenplay for the **Star Wars** sequel before she died.

*Oddly enough, the Martians in the picture above need space suits in order to survive on their own planet. The frame is from **Flight to Mars** (1951), the second most boring movie ever made. The costumes are leftovers from **Destination Moon** (1950). At left is a flying wing from **Conquest of Space** (1955) the sequel to **Destination Moon.** Note the wires that keep the wing in the air.*

A giant bat-rat-spider from
The Angry Red Planet
(1959). The movie was directed
by Ib Melchior and based on a
story by Sid Pink.

Abbott and Costello really only
ended up at the Mardi Gras in
Abbott and Costello Go to
***Mars** (1953). Their space ship*
went haywire and took them on
a runaway ride through New
York and to New Orleans.

A buxom maiden from **Starship Invasions.**

Will Eisner and Lou Fine created this illustration for "Flint Baker and the One-Eyed Monsters of Mars," which appeared in **Planet Comics.**

On the facing page, an astronaut in **Conquest of Space** *(1955) seeks solace in a larger-than-life video doll.* **Conquest's** *producer was veteran George Pal.*

Left: *An artist's conception of Americans landing on the Moon. The ramp on the right side of the space capsule is used in loading and unloading the rover in the center of the picture.*

Above: *A Viking photograph of the surface of Mars. The hollows beside the rocks are evidence of Martian wind.*

CHAPTER THREE

THE SOLAR SYSTEM

The solar system is a big place, with plenty of room for all sorts of alien creatures to cook up evil schemes (and occasionally good ones) directed at the Earth. Over the years, heavenly bodies from the Sun to Pluto have supplied the backgrounds for science fiction on and off the screen.

Stanley Kubrick's masterpiece, *2001: A Space Odyssey*, takes place no farther away from home than the planet Jupiter. Jupiter is the destination of the five astronauts sent to investigate a ubiquitous black monolith that has been puzzling scientists back on Earth. The ultimate mission takes the single surviving astronaut, David Bowman, (Keir Dullea) far beyond Jupiter, but the principal arena of action is more or less our own backyard.

The controversial television series *Space: 1999*, which survived the ratings game for two seasons, began in our solar system, but quickly passed beyond it in the nuclear explosion that sent Moonbase Alpha on its voyage through space. *Space: 1999* brought genuinely sophisticated special effects to television and set high standards for series to follow.

An R2D2-like Drone from
Silent Running *(1971)*
silhouetted against the surface of Saturn.

Facing page: *This drawing by Brad Hamman portrays a traffic jam on an intergalactic highway.*

Left: *Illustration by Elliot Dold for "The Saphrophyte Men of Venus," story by Nat Schachner in* **Astounding Stories,** *October, 1936.*

Above: *Illustration by Frank R. Paul for "Into Plutonian Depths," story by Stanton A. Coblentz in* **Wonder Stories Quarterly,** *Spring, 1931.*

TALES OF WONDER

№3

1/-

THE HORROR
IN THE
TELESCOPE
BY
EDMOND HAMILTON

Venus

Facing page: *A giant robot executioner, who rubs out victims picked by an organization called The Killers, is depicted in this illustration by Ed Valigusky for "The Iron Men of Venus," story by Don Wilcox in* **Amazing Stories,** *February, 1952.*

Left: *In Edmond Hamilton's thriller, dinosaur-like monsters molest nude bathers, under telescopic observation.*

Left: Life on Uranus
*Metal-encased Uranians roll
out the welcome mat for a
gun-toting astronaut from
Earth. The Earthling's space
ship is parked in the
background, flanked by huge,
tree-like crystals. Illustration
by Frank R. Paul on the back
cover of* **Fantastic
Adventures**, *April, 1940.*

Life on Jupiter
*Another Paul illustration of life
on other planets, this time of
Jovians. According to Paul,
the inhabitants of Jupiter have
heavy reptilian bodies,
enabling them to withstand
their planet's estimable gravity.
In this illustration, which
appeared on the back cover of*
Fantastic Adventures *in
January, 1940, an Earthling
makes contact.*

Cover illustration for "The Man from the Atom," which appeared in Science and Invention.

A beautiful maiden is awakened by monsters in Peter Poulton's illustration for a story by Anne McCaffrey in Science Fiction Plus, October, 1953.

The space ark lands on the planet Zyra in George Pal's **When Worlds Collide.** *(1951). The screenplay was based on a story by Edwin Balmer and Philip Wylie.*

A frame from an unproduced 1953 movie, **Dream of the Stars,** *which was intended to be a tour of the solar system with stops at each of the planets. Producer was Morris Scott Dollens.*

Wilma Deering is less frightened than she might be as she falls into the hands of the Zuggs, mindless inhabitants of Saturn, in **Buck Rogers** *(1939). Miss Deering is portrayed by Constance Moore.*

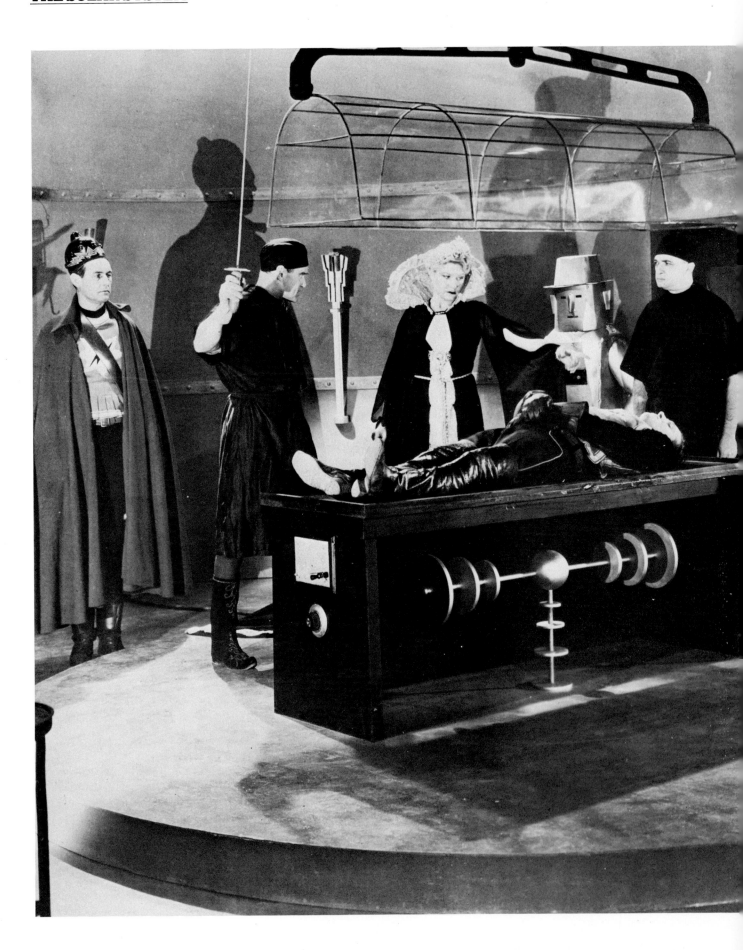

Fire Maidens From Outer Space (1956), *although generally agreed to be one of the worst science fiction movies ever made, was nonetheless the first to use a classical score.*

Left: *The Queen of Murania, who rules the center of the Earth, gives Gene Autry the once-over. This scene is from* **Phantom Empire,** *a Mascot serial.*

THE SOLAR SYSTEM

Left: Planetary nebula in the constellation Aquarius, as seen through the Hale Observatory's 200-inch telescope.

Below: Some basic information about our solar system.

Facing page: An immense and beautiful solar eruption. Such flares are so powerful that they can cause pronounced disturbances in radio communications on Earth.

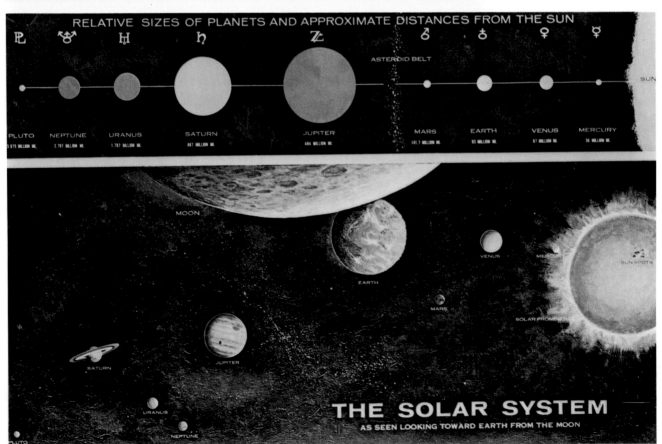

RELATIVE SIZES OF PLANETS AND APPROXIMATE DISTANCES FROM THE SUN

PLUTO	NEPTUNE	URANUS	SATURN	JUPITER	MARS	EARTH	VENUS	MERCURY
3,675 MILLION MI.	2,797 MILLION MI.	1,787 MILLION MI.	887 MILLION MI.	484 MILLION MI.	141.7 MILLION MI.	93 MILLION MI.	67 MILLION MI.	36 MILLION MI.

ASTEROID BELT

SUN

MOON · EARTH · VENUS · MERCURY · MARS · JUPITER · SATURN · URANUS · NEPTUNE · PLUTO · SUN SPOTS · SOLAR PROMINENCE

THE SOLAR SYSTEM
AS SEEN LOOKING TOWARD EARTH FROM THE MOON

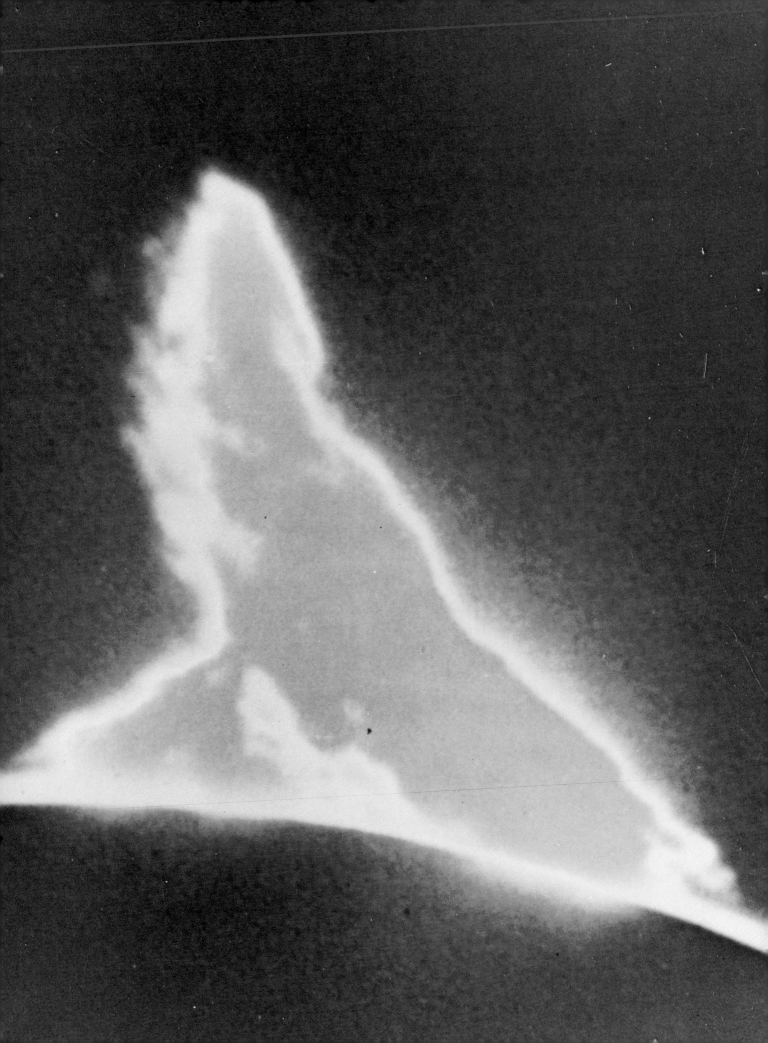

Zsa Zsa Gabor is unmasked in
Queen of Outer Space
*(1958). The action takes place
on Venus.*

Above: *Flash's companion Dale Arden (Carol Hughes) is menaced by a robot built of automotive parts on the planet Mongo in* **Flash Gordon Conquers the Universe.**

Left: *A distinctly phallic "Thing From Venus" captures a pretty girl in this cover illustration from* **Planet Stories.**

Left: *The red rocks of Mars, as photographed by Viking. Note the dust covering parts of the lander.*

Above: A NASA pictorial chart of the Viking mission.

Left:
Charlton Heston is tried by the Ape Elders in **Planet of the Apes** *(1968). In an early scene from the same movie, the space explorers come across the scare crows which mark the boundaries of the forbidden zone.*

CHAPTER FOUR

BEYOND THE SOLAR SYSTEM

Screenwriters feeling hemmed in by the known physical attributes of our corner of the universe have not hesitated to let their minds wander beyond it. Some of the most fantastic planets ever imagined are located far beyond the reaches of our solar system and even of our galaxy.

Mongo, Metaluna, Altair-IV, Ygam, and Terra are just a few of the dozens of bizarre (and sometimes, unfortunately, not so bizarre) imaginary worlds that moviegoers have become accustomed to.

George Lucas's smash hit *Star Wars* added Tatooine, the double-sunned home of Luke Skywalker, and the Death Star, Darth Vader's sinister domain, to the ever-expanding reaches of the imaginary universe.

As scientists' knowledge of space continues to grow, and science-fiction writers struggle to keep a step ahead, the imaginary planets that have become a staple of our imaginations will no doubt become more and more marvelous and position themselves even farther into the Beyond.

Frank R. Paul's cover illustration for "Interplanetary Excursions," a story in **Amazing** *Magazine.*

Facing page: *Artist John Butterfield's conception of a planet inhabited by intelligent insects.*

Facing page: *Two scenes from* **Star Trek.** *Above is the planet Eminar 7 from the "Taste of Armegeddon" episode. Below is a cityscape from "Whom Gods Destroy."*

Left: *Frank Frazetta's illustration for the cover of* **Tales of the Incredible** *from Ballantine Books.*

*The war-torn surface of the planet Metaluna in **This Island Earth** (1954). The Earthlings in the center are trying to make it to the Metalunan ship that will ferry them to safety, unless the invaders from Zagon get in the way.*

*Two more scenes from **This Island Earth.** Above is an overhead view of the subterranean city pictured on the facing page. At left is the Metalunan ship, which is in distinct danger of connecting with a Zagon missile.*

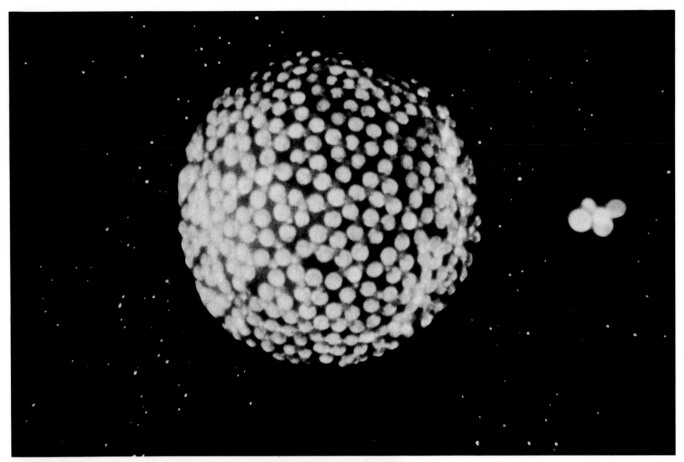

*Two shots from the **Star Trek** episode "The Corbomite Maneuver." The evil looking sphere in both pictures is the huge alien ship commanded by Balok. The tiny vessel in the foreground of the picture at left is the good old Enterprise, in grave danger as usual.*

More **Star Trek.** *Above, a fleet of Klingon ships surrounds the Enterprise. Below, Kirk confronts Spock's evil double in the Savage Universe that was the subject of "Mirror Mirror."*

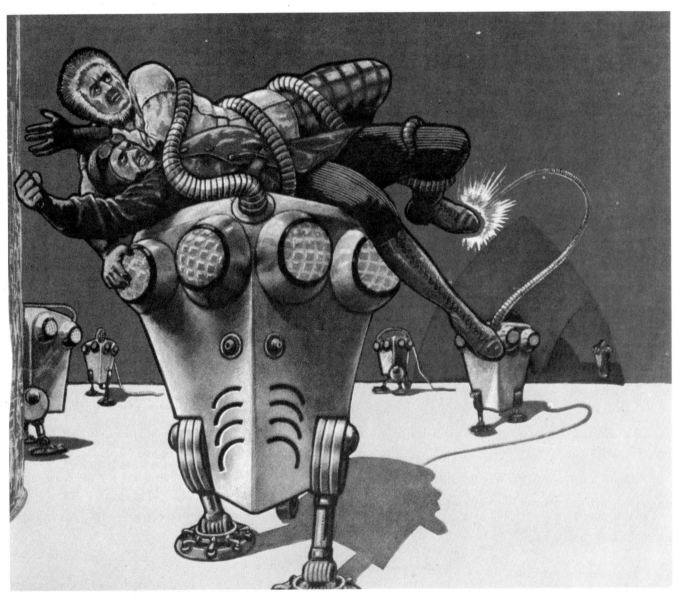

*Above: An illustration by Frank R. Paul from **Thrilling Wonder Stories**, 1933.*
Left: Adventure in space as portrayed by a Soviet artist.
*Facing page: Underwater action in the **Flash Gordon** comic strip, created by **Alex Raymond.***

MING'S AIR FLEET APPROACHES THE UNDERSEA CITY OF CORALIA.............

THE "Z" RAY LOCATED THEIR CITY, JUST AS WE EXPECTED!

SHALL WE RELEASE THE SUPER-DEPTH BOMBS, CAPTAIN?

SUDDENLY, MAGNETO-RAYS FROM THE OCEAN DEPTHS SEIZE THE ROCKET SHIPS AND DRAG THEM TO THEIR DOOM!

FROM A LONELY OUTPOST ON THE SEA BOTTOM, QUEEN UNDINA GLOATS OVER HER VICTORY.............

SPLENDID WORK, TRITON! THAT'LL TEACH MING BETTER MANNERS!

I CAN'T BELIEVE MING INTENDED TO DEFEAT YOU FROM THE AIR, UNDINA...... MAY I BORROW A SPEED-SLED FOR A LITTLE SCOUTING?

RACING AROUND CORALIA, FLASH RUNS INTO MING'S SUBMARINE FLEET!

Lovely Barbarella.

*Above is the pleasure palace that causes so much trouble in **Barbarella.** On the facing page, the heroine is rescued from prison by Tigar the Blind Angel (John Philip Law).*

Jane Fonda in her birthday suit tries out the torture chamber.

*A robot runs amok in this famous illustration by Kelly Freas for **Astounding Fiction.***

Facing page: *Dr. Smith (Jonathan Harris) criticizes the robot's painting ability in an episode of **Lost in Space.** In case anyone is interested, the man inside the robot is Bob May.*

BEYOND THE SOLAR SYSTEM

There are as many varieties of space vehicles as there are species of aliens. At right, Anne Francis tries out Morbius's land rover in a scene from **Forbidden Planet** (1956) Below, the puppet cast of the television show **Supercar** (filmed in Supermarionation) ready their vehicle for a trip.

Above: *Dr. Smith, in trouble as usual, is transported Gulliver-style by a band of miniature robots.*

Below: *The space family Robinson's multi-purpose rover.*

Left: *Altair-IV's Klystron relays, immensely powerful sources of energy.*

Above: *"City in the Sky" from a 1972* **Analog** *magazine. Could this cover illustration have provided the inspiration for the mother ship in* **Close Encounters?**

Above: *A United Planets cruiser prepares to land on Altair-IV in* **Forbidden Planet** *(1956).*

Below: *The crew disembarks from the above.*

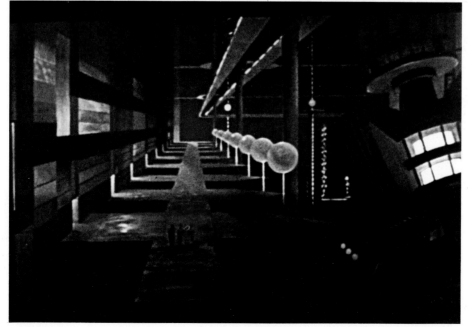

Above: *Robbie the Robot prepares to meet the travelers pictured on the facing page.*

Below: *The incredible Krel dynamoes, with "20,000 miles of Klystron relays," deep under the surface of Altair-IV. The matte painting used in this shot was designed by Disney artist Josh Meador.*

One of the monsters that came from the **Outer Limits** and captivated TV viewers from 1963 to 1965. The show was produced by Joseph Stefano, who wrote the screenplay for Alfred Hitchcock's **Psycho.**

Facing page: Kirk and Spock surrounded by women who do not wish them well. The episode was called "Mudd's Women."

Above: Ruth Buzzi and Jim Nabors cavort in "The Lost Saucer," a short-lived television series about an intergalactic schoolbus.

*Billy Pilgrim (Michael Saks), the man who became unstuck in time, relaxes with his dog in their cage at the zoo run by the invisible inhabitants of Tralfamador in Kurt Vonnegut Jr.'s **Slaughterhouse-Five** (1971).*

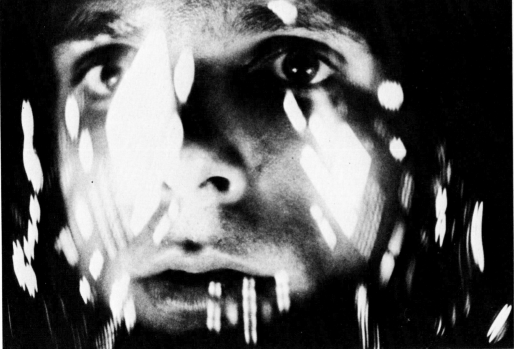

The Star Gate

Above: *Astronaut Bowman (Keir Dullea) faces the monolith, at the end of* **2001.**

Left: *Bowman passes through the star gate.*

Top: *The perplexing view from the space pod.*

Bottom: *Passing through the star gate. Special effects by Douglas Trumball.*

C3PO and his ancestors

Facing page: Pre-production painting by Ralph McQuarrie for the 1978 TV series "Battlestar Galactica," effects by John (**Star Wars**) Dykstra.

Above: C3PO himself, accompanied by R2D2.

Left: A robot from an old Cover of **Astounding** magazine who bears an astounding resemblance to the metallic crowd-pleaser from **Star Wars.**

*The Jawas and their sand crawler, from **Star Wars.***

Overleaf:
*A pre-production painting by Ralph McQuarrie for **Star Wars.***

ACKNOWLEDGEMENTS

We wish to thank the following sources for photographs and artwork. If there are any emendations or ommissions, contact the publishers, and corrections will be made in subsequent editions.

ABC-TV: 149

Academy Film Stills Archive: 9T, 9M, 11, 90T, 140B

David Allen: 29B

Allied Artists: 116

Amazing Stories: 6R, 104, 122

American Internation Pictures: 17B, 95T

Analog Science Fact & Fiction Magazine: 27B, 59 Inset, 86T, 102-103, 124, 138, 143 Inset,155B

Ballantine Books,Inc.: 127

Better Publications,Inc.: (c) 1948 by Better Publications,Inc.: 109

Edgar Rice Burroughs,Inc.: 12, 84, 85, 92B

John Butterfield: 123

Bob Clampett: (c)1978 by Bob Clampett. World Rights Reserved: 72T&B

Columbia Pictures: From the Columbia Pictures Release **Close Encounters of the Third Kind** (c)1978 Columbia Pictures Inc.: 1 (alien figure), 19, 23B, 66-67; From the Columbia Pictures Release **Explorers On The Moon, The Adventures of Tintin** by Herge Art © Casterman, Paris. Text © by Methuen, London. Little Brown Co., Boston : 6L, 40T

First Men in the Moon (c)1964 Columbia Pictures Inc.: 25B,35,49

Morris Scott Dollens: 110B

Famous Fantastic Mysteries: 76, 86B

Famous Funnies: 92T

Fantastic Adventures: 106, 107

Virgil Finlay: 125

Frank Kelly Freas: 138

William M. Gaines: Weird Science, (c)1979 by William M. Gaines: 62, 63, 91T&B

Hale Observatory: 114T

Brad Hamman: 101

ITC Entertainment Ltd.: 23T, 30, 52T&B, 53, 70

Courtesy King Features Syndicate: 133

Tom Kowal: cover,31

Jeff Kronen: 71

Mammoth Films: **Flesh Gordon**, Mammoth Films Inc.,1972: 28

Mascot Films: 112

MGM: From MGM Release **Forbidden Planet**, (c)1956 Loew's Incorporated: 140T, 142-143, 144T&B, 145T&B; MGM Release **The Time Machine**, (c)1960 Metro-Goldwyn-Mayer Inc.: 16TL, 29M; From MGM Release **2001: A Space Odyssey, (c)1968 Metro-Goldwyn-Mayer Inc.: 46-47, 64-65, 68-69, 152T&B, 153&B**

Monogram Films: 94T

Museum of Modern Art Film/Stills Archive: 32-33, 33 Inset, 34B, 36T&B

National Aeronautics and Space Administration: 3, 7, 9B, 20B, 22, 40B, 41, 43 Inset, 48-49, 50-51, 51 Inset, 60-61, 74T&B, 75, 78-79, 98-99, 99, 114B, 115, 118, 119

National Air and Space Museum of the Smithsonian Instituion: 44B, 54-55, 88, 108T, 119 Inset, 132B

New York Public Library Picture Collection: 5R, 34T

George Pal Productions/Eagle-Lion Films: 2, 42-43, 44T, 56-57

Paramount Picture: From Paramount Pictures Release Barbarella, (c)1968 Paramount Pictures Inc.: 15, 24, 134, 135, 136-137; From the Paramount Pictures Release The Conquest of Space, (c)1955 Paramount Pictures Inc.: 94B, 96-97; From the Paramount Pictures Release When Worlds Collide, (c)1951 Paramount Pictures Inc.: 110T; From Paramount Television Production Star Trek (NBC-Norway Productions): 16TR, 16B, 18, 20TR, 26, 58-59, 126T&B, 130T&B, 131T&B, 148

Planet Comics: 97B

Planet Stories:87, 93, 117B

Science Fiction Plus: 77, 108B

Chris Spollen: 4

Startling Stories: 38

Tales of Wonder: 89, 105

Thrilling Wonder Stories: 132T

Twentieth Century-Fox: From 20th Century-Fox Release **Planet of the Apes, (c)1968 Twentieth Century-Fox Film Corporation: 120-121, 121 Inset; From Twentieth Century-Fox Release Star Wars** (c)1977 Twentieth Century-Fox Film Corporation: 27T, 155T, 156-157, 158-159; From the 20th Century-Fox Release **The Day the Earth Stood Still**, (c)1951 Twentieth Century-Fox Film Corporation: 20TL; From Twentieth Century-Fox Television Production **Lost In Space** (Irwin Allen, CBS); 139, 141T&B

United Artists: From the United Artists Release **Things to Come**, (c)1936, United Artists Corporation: 13; From the United Artists Television Production **The Outer Limits** (ABC Daystar-Villa di Stefano): 25T, 29T, 146-147

Universal Pictures: From Universal Pictures Film **Abbott & Costello Go To Mars**, (c)1953 Universal Pictures Inc.: 95B; From Universal Pictures Film **Buck Rogers**, (c)1939 Universal Pictures Inc.: 21L, 111; From Universal Pictures Film **Flash Gordon**, (c)1936 Universal Pictures Inc.: 17T; From Universal Pictures Film **Flash Gordon Conquers the Universe**, (c)1940 Universal Pictures Inc.: 21R, 117T; From Universal Pictures Film **Flash Gordon's Trip to Mars, (c)1938 Universal Pictures Inc.: 80, 81, 82-83; Universal Pictures Film Silent Running**, (c)1971 Universal Pictures Inc.: 100; Universal Pictures Film **Slaughterhouse-Five**, (C)1971 Universal Pictures Inc.: 150-151; From Universal Pictures Film **This Island Earth**, (c) 1954 Universal Pictures Inc.: 10, 128, 129T&B; Universal Television Production **Battlestar Galactica**: 154

Warner Brother: Warner Bros. Film **Moon Zero-Two** (Hammer Films, 1969): 45, 61 Inset; Warner Bros. Film **Starship Invasions**, (c)1977 Warner Communications Inc.: 97T

Wonder Stories: 39

Wonder Stories Quarterly: 103 Inset

Zimgor Productions/Lippert Distributing: 5L